Weimaraner Dogs as Pets

Weimaraner Breeding, Where to Buy, Types, Care, Temperament, Cost, Health, Showing, Grooming, Diet and Much More Included!

By Lolly Brown

Copyrights and Trademarks

Disclaimer and Legal Notice

Foreword

The Weimaraner dog breed is known for its athletic build, its silver-grey coat, and its energetic personality. Developed as a hunting breed, the Weimaraner has excellent stamina and they are well-rounded hunters, skilled in tracking, pointing, and retrieving. These dogs are not the right choice for everyone, but they can be a wonderful pet if you have the time to dedicate to this active and energetic breed. Weimaraner dogs bond very closely with their owners and, with proper training and socialization, they make wonderful family pets.

If you are thinking about getting a Weimaraner dog, you would be wise to learn everything you can about this unique and beautiful breed - that is where this book comes in. In this book you will find a wealth of useful information about the Weimaraner dog breed including details tips for care. In reading this book you will learn everything you need to know to decide whether or not the Weimaraner is the right breed for you and, if it is, you will be well on your way to becoming the best dog owner you can be!

So, if you are ready to learn what you need to know about the Weimaraner dog breed, simply turn the page and keep reading!

Table of Contents

Introduction

When you picture the Weimaraner breed, you probably imagine a lithe, athletic dog with a gorgeous silver-blue coat. Not only is the Weimaraner an attractive and athletic breed, but these dogs are also talented hunters. The Weimaraner has excellent stamina and it is a well-rounded hunter, skilled in tracking, pointing, and retrieving. If you are looking for a skilled hunting breed, the Weimaraner is definitely an option to consider. It is important to remember, however, that training a hunting dog is a big responsibility – a major commitment of time and dedication.

Weimaraner dogs are not the right choice for everyone, but they can be a wonderful pet if you have the time to dedicate to this active and energetic breed. These dogs do have a tendency to develop behavioral problems such as separation anxiety but, with proper training and socialization, they make wonderful family pets. The Weimaraner is a gentle and loving breed that bonds very closely with its owners and they will do everything they can to become your very best friend.

If you are thinking about getting a Weimaraner dog, you would be wise to learn everything you can about this beautiful and energetic breed – that is where this book comes in. Within the pages of this book you will find a wealth of useful information about the Weimaraner dog breed including details tips for care. In reading this book you will learn everything you need to know to decide whether or not the Weimaraner is the right breed for you and, if it is, you will be well on your way to becoming the best dog owner you can be!

So, if you are ready to learn what you need to know about the Weimaraner dog breed, simply open up this book and keep reading!

Glossary of Dog Terms

AKC – American Kennel Club, the largest purebred dog registry in the United States

Almond Eye – Referring to an elongated eye shape rather than a rounded shape

Apple Head – A round-shaped skull

Balance – A show term referring to all of the parts of the dog, both moving and standing, which produce a harmonious image

Beard – Long, thick hair on the dog's underjaw

Best in Show – An award given to the only undefeated dog left standing at the end of judging

Bitch – A female dog

Bite – The position of the upper and lower teeth when the dog's jaws are closed; positions include level, undershot, scissors, or overshot

Blaze – A white stripe running down the center of the face between the eyes

Board – To house, feed, and care for a dog for a fee

Breed – A domestic race of dogs having a common gene pool and characterized appearance/function

Breed Standard – A published document describing the look, movement, and behavior of the perfect specimen of a particular breed

Buff – An off-white to gold coloring

Clip – A method of trimming the coat in some breeds

Coat – The hair covering of a dog; some breeds have two coats, and outer coat and undercoat; also known as a double coat. Examples of breeds with double coats include German Shepherd, Siberian Husky, Akita, etc.

Condition – The health of the dog as shown by its skin, coat, behavior, and general appearance

Crate – A container used to house and transport dogs; also called a cage or kennel

Crossbreed (Hybrid) – A dog having a sire and dam of two different breeds; cannot be registered with the AKC

Dam (bitch) – The female parent of a dog;

Dock – To shorten the tail of a dog by surgically removing the end part of the tail.

Double Coat – Having an outer weather-resistant coat and a soft, waterproof coat for warmth; see above.

Drop Ear – An ear in which the tip of the ear folds over and hangs down; not prick or erect

Entropion – A genetic disorder resulting in the upper or lower eyelid turning in

Fancier – A person who is especially interested in a particular breed or dog sport

Fawn – A red-yellow hue of brown

Feathering – A long fringe of hair on the ears, tail, legs, or body of a dog

Groom – To brush, trim, comb or otherwise make a dog's coat neat in appearance

Heel – To command a dog to stay close by its owner's side

Hip Dysplasia – A condition characterized by the abnormal formation of the hip joint

Inbreeding – The breeding of two closely related dogs of one breed

Kennel – A building or enclosure where dogs are kept

Litter – A group of puppies born at one time

Markings – A contrasting color or pattern on a dog's coat

Mask – Dark shading on the dog's foreface

Mate – To breed a dog and a bitch

Neuter – To castrate a male dog or spay a female dog

Pads – The tough, shock-absorbent skin on the bottom of a dog's foot

Parti-Color – A coloration of a dog's coat consisting of two or more definite, well-broken colors; one of the colors must be white

Pedigree – The written record of a dog's genealogy going back three generations or more

Pied – A coloration on a dog consisting of patches of white and another color

Prick Ear – Ear that is carried erect, usually pointed at the tip of the ear

Puppy – A dog under 12 months of age

Purebred – A dog whose sire and dam belong to the same breed and who are of unmixed descent

Saddle – Colored markings in the shape of a saddle over the back; colors may vary

Shedding – The natural process whereby old hair falls off the dog's body as it is replaced by new hair growth.

Sire – The male parent of a dog

Smooth Coat – Short hair that is close-lying

Spay – The surgery to remove a female dog's ovaries, rendering her incapable of breeding

Trim – To groom a dog's coat by plucking or clipping

Undercoat – The soft, short coat typically concealed by a longer outer coat

Wean – The process through which puppies transition from subsisting on their mother's milk to eating solid food

Whelping – The act of birthing a litter of puppies

Chapter One: Understanding Weimaraners

Before you can truly decide whether or not the Weimaraner is the right breed for you, you need to learn as much as you can about these beautiful dogs. Weimaraners can make good family pets for the right owners, but they are not always the best choice. In this chapter you will learn the basics about Weimaraner dogs including key facts about their personality and temperament to help you make your decision. In the next chapter you will receive some practical tips about owning a Weimaraner as well – these two chapters combined will help you make your choice.

Facts About Weimaraner Dogs

Some dog breeds have such a distinct appearance that it is easy to identify them – the Weimaraner is one of those breeds. These dogs have long, muscular legs and an athletic build, not to mention a silver-blue coat that makes them stand out in a crowd. This breed is not small by any means, though they are usually fairly slim. Weimaraners were originally bred to hunt large game but eventually came to be used as an all-purpose gun dog, so these dogs are highly versatile and skilled in hunting.

When it comes to the Weimaraner's appearance, you can expect these dogs to grow between 23 and 27 inches (58.5 to 68.5 cm) tall and to weigh between 55 and 90 pounds (25 to 41 kg) at maturity. Females of the breed are generally a little smaller than males, but they are equally skilled in hunting. Traditionally, dogs of this breed have their tails docked to no longer than 6 inches (15.2 cm) but because tail docking has been outlawed in many countries (and because some consider the practice cruelty to animals), it is becoming increasingly more common to see this breed with its natural whip-like tail.

The Weimaraner is easy to identify by its silver-blue color, but you may not realize that this breed comes with two different coat types. The ideal type for the Weimaraner exhibits a short, close coat that is hard and smooth to the touch. Though silver-blue is the most common coloration, the coat color may vary from charcoal-blue to blue-grey or even mouse-grey. It is possible for Weimaraners to be born with black coats or with long hair, but both of these characteristics are considered grounds for disqualification by the United Kennel Club. The AKC still recognizes these dogs as purebred, but they are not eligible for show.

Though the Weimaraner's coat is traditionally very short, it is extremely low-maintenance. The coat does shed, but because the breed doesn't have an undercoat it isn't a significant concern. Regular brushing will help to reduce shedding for this breed and it will also help to keep the dog's coat silky and smooth by distributing the natural oils produced by glands in the dog's skin. In areas where the coat is particularly thin (such as inside the ears or on the lips), the skin color may be more pink than grey. Because these dogs don't have a thick coat or an undercoat, they do not tend to do well in extreme cold.

Because the Weimaraner was developed as a hunting breed, these dogs are very active and require a good deal of daily exercise. This breed has excellent stamina and endurance, so a brisk jog is the best way to give them their daily dose of exercise – Weimaraners will also enjoy having free time to run and play in a fenced yard. This breed is also very smart, so they require mental stimulation in addition to physical exercise. Training is a good way to challenge your Weimaraner, though you can also play games with him or give him interactive toys to play with.

Another consequence of the breed's hunting background is a strong prey drive. Weimaraners were originally bred to hunt large game but as that sport declined, they came to be used for smaller game like rabbits. This being the case, you should be wary of leaving your Weimaraner alone around small household pets like cats and birds – they may even have trouble with small dogs. If you plan to keep your Weimaraner with other pets, early socialization and training will be extremely important. These dogs should also be supervised around young children, though they can get along with older children who know how to handle a dog.

In terms of training, each Weimaraner is different. In general, this is an intelligent breed that generally responds well to training but their independent nature can sometimes lead them to become headstrong. Weimaraners are sometimes tricky to housetrain and they require firm and consistent training throughout their lives. This breed is prone to separation anxiety so they need plenty of training to avoid problem behaviors. They can also be somewhat suspicious of strangers, even to the point of aggressiveness if they aren't trained and socialized.

With an owner who is experienced in caring for and training dogs – and for families who have the time to devote to high exercise needs and lifelong training – the Weimaraner can make a good family pet. These dogs are not, however, recommended for in experienced dog owners or for families looking for a low-maintenance or outdoor dog. This breed can live to an average of 11 to 14 years and they are generally healthy but, like all dogs, can be prone to certain diseases. The most common health problems affecting the Weimaraner breed include hip dysplasia, gastric dilation volvulus, von Willebrand's Disease, distichiasis, entropion, hypothyroidism, progressive retinal atrophy, and skin allergies. Responsible breeding practices can reduce the risk for many of these diseases.

Summary of Weimaraner Facts

Pedigree: developed during the 19th century from various breeds including the Bloodhound, English Pointer, German Shorthaired Pointer and the blue Great Dane

AKC Group: Sporting Group

Breed Size: Medium

Height: 23 to 27 inches (58.5 to 68.5 cm)

Weight: 55 to 90 pounds (25 to 41 kg)

Coat Length: short

Coat Texture: coarse, hard and smooth

Color: silver-grey is most common but may range from charcoal-blue to blue-grey or even mouse-grey

Eyes and Nose: grey, blue-grey, or amber

Ears: drop ears; large, very thin

Tail: traditionally docked to maximum of 6 inches (15.2 cm); may be left natural; long and whip-like

Temperament: high-energy, intelligent, independent, high-strung, people-oriented

Strangers: often suspicious of strangers and may act aggressively unless they are trained and socialized from an early age

Children: may not be a good choice for young children; can get along with other children who are accustomed to dogs

Other Dogs: depends on the dog; some have a low tolerance for other dogs (especially small dogs) but this problem can often be remedied with training and socialization if started at an early age

Training: intelligent and very trainable; they can learn quickly but need constant stimulation to avoid boredom; prone to separation anxiety

Exercise Needs: bred for excellent stamina and endurance so they have high exercise needs; brisk daily jog is recommended along with time to run in a fenced yard

Health Conditions: hip dysplasia, gastric dilation volvulus, von Willebrand's Disease, distichiasis, entropion, hypothyroidism, progressive retinal atrophy, skin allergies

Lifespan: average 11 to 14 years

Weimaraner Breed History

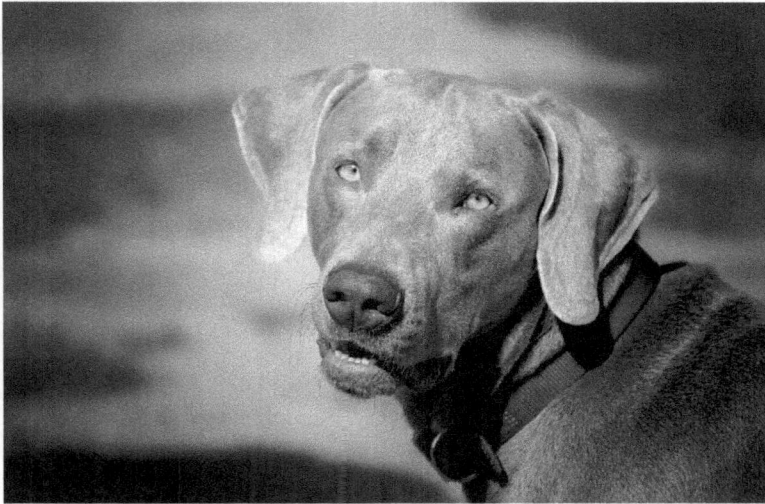

The Weimaraner is not an ancient breed, but his development does date back to the early 19th century. The breed was developed at the Weimar court (hence the name) in what is now Germany. During the early 19th century, noblemen needed a hunting dog that had great courage, strong scenting ability, excellent stamina, and impressive speed. The dog also needed to stay close to the hunter during the search for game and remain by his side as a faithful companion in the home.

Early specimens of the breed were known as Weimar Pointers and they were developed through the crossing of various hunting and pointing breeds such as the Bloodhound, the German Shorthaired Pointer, the English Pointer, and the blue Great Dane. Originally, the breed was used to hunt large game like boar and deer but, as large game became more and more scarce, the breed adapted to hunting smaller game such as rabbits, foxes and gamebirds. This is how the Weimaraner came to be such a skilled and versatile hunting breed today.

In 1897, an exclusive Weimaraner breed club was formed in Germany and the sale of Weimaraner puppies was reserved for members of the club. There were also strict guidelines for breeding Weimaraners that all breeders were expected to follow. The first specimens of the breed were imported in the United States by Howard Knight, an American sportsman, in 1929. The first dogs the German club gave him were both desexed because they were so dedicated to protecting the breed but Knight eventually came into possession of three intact females and a male puppy in 1938.

The Weimaraner Club of America was formed in 1942 and other breeders shortly joined Knight in his quest to develop and show the breed. The AKC recognized the Weimaraner in 1942 and the breed made its formal debut at the Westminster Kennel Club Show the next year. Many specimens of the breed were sent from German to the U.S. during World War II and as American servicemen returned home they also brought their Weimaraners with them. This sparked an increase in popularity for the breed in the United States which continued until the breed was named the 12th most popular breed in the U.S. in the 1950s.

Unfortunately, the sudden increase in popularity for the Weimaraner breed led to a great deal of irresponsible breeding and the quality of the breed fell drastically. Another consequence of irresponsible breeding was the development of temperament problems – some of which are still present in the breed today. The popularity of Weimaraner declined steadily throughout the 1970s and 80s until a small group of breeders sought to restore the breed during the 1990s. Today, the Weimaraner once again has become one of the most popular breeds in the U.S., ranked among the top 30 of nearly 200 AKC-recognized breeds.

Chapter Two: Things to Know Before Getting a Weimaraner

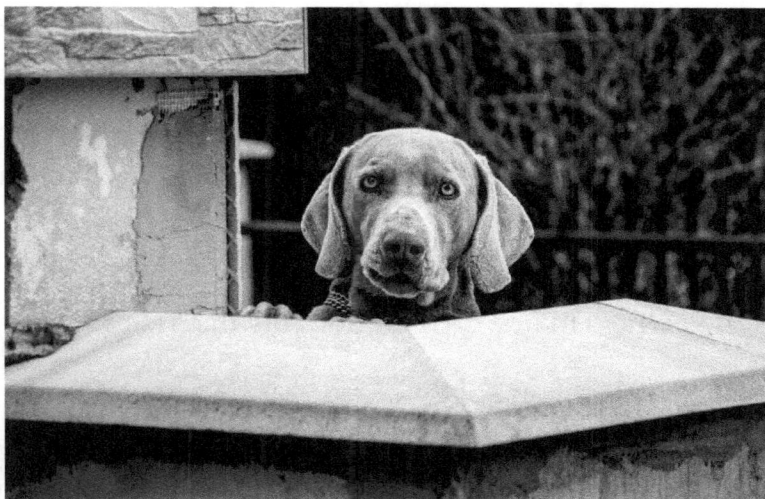

The Weimaraner is a beautiful dog and a talented hunter, but it may not be the right fit for everyone. In addition to considering what you learned about the breed in the previous chapter, you should also think about the practical aspects of owning a Weimaraner. Together, these two chapters will help you to truly determine whether or not the Weimaraner is the best breed for you. If it is, you'll find the information in the rest of this book quite handy as you prepare for your new dog!

Do You Need a License?

The first thing you need to think about before you bring home a new pet is whether it is legal to keep one in your area. Few areas have rules prohibiting dog ownership, but there may be other laws you have to keep in mind. For example, some areas require dog owners to license their dogs while others do not. In the United States, there are no federal requirements for dog licensing – it is determined at the state level. While some states do not, most states require dog owners to license their dogs on an annual basis.

When you apply for a dog license you will have to submit proof that your dog has been given a rabies vaccine. Dog licenses in the United States cost about $25 (£16.25) per year and they can be renewed annually when you renew your dog's rabies vaccine. Even if your state doesn't require you to license your dog it is still a good idea because it will help someone to identify him if he gets lost so they can return him to you.

In the United Kingdom, licensing requirements for dog owners are a little bit different. The U.K. requires that all dog owners license their dogs and the license can be renewed every twelve months. The cost to license your dog in the U.K. is similar to the U.S. but you do not have to have your dog vaccinated against rabies. In fact, rabies does not exist in the U.K. because it was eradicated through careful control measures. If you travel with your dog to or from the U.K., you will have to obtain a special animal moving license and your dog may have to undergo a period of quarantine to make sure he doesn't carry disease into the country.

How Many Weimaraner Dogs Should You Keep?

Once you have determined whether it is legal to keep a dog in your area and if you need a license to do so, you can start to think about whether you should get just one Weimaraner or if you might be better off with two. Some dog breeds are very social and do not like to be left alone. In cases like this, dog owners often decide to get two dogs so that they can keep each other company. The Weimaraner is not necessarily one of these dogs. Weimaraners are trained to hunt independently and they can sometimes be aggressive around smaller dogs.

Many Weimaraners need extra training and socialization just to get along with other dogs so you should not assume that getting a second dog will be the right move for your Weimaraner. Weimaraners are subject to separation anxiety and they can develop problem behaviors when left alone for too long, but they prefer the company of people over the company of dogs. If you don't have the time to dedicate to keeping a Weimaraner happy, you should consider another breed.

Do Weimaraner Dogs Get Along with Other Pets?

In the same way that you need to be careful about keeping a Weimaraner around other dogs, you also have to be careful about keeping one with other household pets. If you think back to the second chapter of this book you will remember that Weimaraners were developed during the late 19th century to hunt large game like bear, boar, and deer. Once hunting for these animals fell out of style, however, Weimaraners were adapted to smaller game. This being the case, most Weimaraners have a strong prey drive.

Many Weimaraner owners have made the mistake of assuming that their dog will get along with other household pets only to discover that their dog chases their cat, other dogs, or even their young children around the house. While socialization and training can help to curb these behaviors, it is best to simply not put your Weimaraner in a situation where this type of problem could develop. Weimaraners do best in single-dog households, though some can get along with other dogs of similar size if they are raised together from a young age.

How Much Does it Cost to Keep a Weimaraner?

In addition to thinking about whether your Weimaraner will get along with your current pets and your lifestyle, you should also think about how much it will cost to keep a Weimaraner as a pet. The costs of keeping a dog involve more than just the purchase price for a puppy – you also have to think about recurring expenses for food, training, and veterinary care. In this section you will receive an overview of the initial costs and the recurring monthly costs involved in Weimaraner ownership. Unless you are able to comfortably cover all of these costs, the Weimaraner may not be the right dog breed for you.

Initial Costs

The initial costs for keeping a Weimaraner as a pet include those costs that you must cover before you can bring your dog home. Some of the initial costs you will need to cover include your dog's crate, food/water bowls, toys and accessories, microchipping, initial vaccinations, spay/neuter surgery and supplies for grooming and nail clipping – it also includes the cost of the dog itself. <u>You will find an overview of each of these costs as well as an estimate for each cost in the following pages</u>:

Purchase Price – If you are going to buy a puppy, you should take the time to do your research so that you find a responsible breeder. You do not want to skimp and end up buying from a backyard breeder because there is a high risk that your Weimaraner puppy could be carrying a genetic disease. It will cost more to buy from an AKC- or Kennel Club-registered breeder, but it will be worth it in the end. The average cost for a Weimaraner puppy from a quality breeder is about $1,200 (£1,080), though the actual price could vary several hundred dollars in either direction according to breeding quality.

Do not pay this price unless it is a purebred Weimaraner. If you do not particularly care about your dog's pedigree, you can save money by adopting a Weimaraner from a rescue agency or shelter. The average cost to adopt a dog is about $150 (£135), and dogs from shelters are generally already spayed/neutered and up to date on vaccinations.

Crate – Weimaraners have a bit of an independent streak and they can sometimes be tricky to housetrain, but crate training is generally recognized as the best method of training for this breed. Your puppy's crate will become his personal space where he can relax and take a nap if he needs to. Because Weimaraner's grow fairly large, you may need to purchase one crate for your puppy and then buy a second crate once he reaches adulthood. The average cost for a small crate is about $30 (£19.50).

Food/Water Bowls – For one Weimaraner you will need at least one food bowl and one water bowl. The cost for these items depends on the size and quality, but you should buy something made from either stainless steel or ceramic because these materials are easier to clean. Plan to spend about $20 (£18) on food and water bowls for your new puppy.

Toys – The Weimaraner is a very high-energy breed who requires a lot of exercise as well as mental stimulation throughout the day. Giving your dog an assortment of toys (including some puzzle toys or interactive toys) may help to keep his high energy levels at bay. You should plan to start your puppy off with a variety of toys until you learn what kind he likes. Plan to budget an initial cost of about $50 (£32.50) for your puppy's first toys.

Microchipping – In the United States and United Kingdom there are no federal or state requirements saying that you have to have your dog microchipped, but it is a very good idea. Your Weimaraner could slip out of his collar on a walk or lose his ID tag. If someone finds him without identification, they can take him to a shelter to have his microchip scanned. A microchip is something that is implanted under your dog's skin and it carries a number that is linked to your contact information. The procedure takes just a few minutes to perform and it only costs about $30 (£19.50) in most cases.

Initial Vaccinations – During your puppy's first year of life, he will require a number of different vaccinations. If you purchase your puppy from a reputable breeder, he might already have had a few but you'll still need more over the next few months as well as booster shots each year. You should budget about $50 (£32.50) for initial vaccinations just to be prepared.

Spay/Neuter Surgery – If you don't plan to breed your Weimaraner you should have him or her neutered or spayed before 6 months of age. The cost for this surgery will vary depending where you go and on the sex of your dog. If you go to a traditional veterinary surgeon, the cost for spay/neuter surgery could be very high but you can save money by going to a veterinary clinic. The average cost for neuter surgery is $50 to $100 (£32.50 - £65) and spay surgery costs about $100 to $200 (£65 - £130).

Supplies/Accessories – In addition to purchasing your Weimaraner's crate and food/water bowls, you should also purchase some basic grooming supplies as well as a leash and collar. The cost for these items will vary depending on the quality, but you should budget about $50 (£32.50) for these extra costs.

Initial Costs for Weimaraners		
Cost	One Dog	Two Dogs
Purchase Price	$150 to $1,200 (£135 to £1,080)	$300 to $2,400 (£270 to £2,160)
Crate	$30 (£19.50)	$60 (£39)
Food/Water Bowl	$20 (£18)	$40 (£36)
Toys	$50 (£32.50)	$50 (£32.50)
Microchipping	$30 (£19.50)	$60 (£39)
Vaccinations	$50 (£32.50)	$100 (£65)
Spay/Neuter	$50 to $200 (£32.50 - £130)	$100 to $400 (£65 - £260)
Accessories	$50 (£32.50)	$100 (£90)
Total	$430 to $1,630 (£387 – £1,467)	$810 to $3,210 (£729 – £2,890)

*Costs may vary depending on location
**U.K. prices based on an estimated exchange of $1 = £0.90

Monthly Costs

The monthly costs for keeping a Weimaraner as a pet include those costs which recur on a monthly basis. The most important monthly cost for keeping a dog is, of course, food. In addition to food, however, you'll also need to think about things like grooming costs, annual license renewal, toy replacements, and veterinary exams. You will find an overview of each of these costs as well as an estimate for each cost in the following pages:

Food and Treats – Feeding your Weimaraner puppy a healthy diet is very important for his health and wellness – you want to give him the nutrients he needs to grow but you shouldn't overfeed him because growing too quickly could cause health problems. A high-quality diet for dogs is not cheap, so you should be prepared to spend around $35 (£31.50) on a large bag of high-quality dog food which will last you about a month. You should also include a monthly budget of about $10 (£6.50) for treats, perhaps more during your initial puppy training.

Grooming Costs – The Weimaraner has a short, rough coat that doesn't require a lot of maintenance. For the most part, brushing your dog a few times a week should be enough to keep shedding under control but you may want to have your dog professionally groomed once or twice a year to keep his skin and coat in good condition. The average cost for a professional grooming visit is about $50 (£32.50). If you budget for two visits per year, it averages to a monthly grooming cost around $8 (£7).

License Renewal – The cost to license your Weimaraner will generally be about $25 (£16.25) and you can renew the license for the same price each year. License renewal cost divided over 12 months is about $2 (£1.30) per month.

Veterinary Exams – In order to keep your Weimaraner healthy you should take him to the veterinarian about every six months after he passes puppyhood. You might have to take him more often for the first 12 months to make sure he gets his vaccines on time. The average cost for a vet visit is about $40 (£26) so, if you have two visits per year, it averages to about $7 (£4.55) per month.

Other Costs – In addition to the monthly costs for your Weimaraner's food, grooming, license renewal, and vet visits there are also some other cost you might have to pay occasionally. These costs might include things like replacements for worn-out toys, a larger collar as your puppy grows, cleaning products, and more. You should budget about $15 (£9.75) per month for extra costs.

Monthly Costs for Weimaraner Dogs		
Cost	One Dog	Two Dogs
Food and Treats	S45 (£40.50)	$90 (£81)
Grooming Costs	$8 (£7)	$16 (£14)
License Renewal	$2 (£1.30)	$4 (£3.60)
Veterinary Exams	$7 (£4.55)	$14 (£12.60)
Other Costs	$15 (£9.75)	$30 (£19.50)
Total	$77 (£6p)	$154 (£139)

*Costs may vary depending on location
**U.K. prices based on an estimated exchange of $1 = £0.90

What are the Pros and Cons of Weimaraner Dogs?

By now you should have a deeper understanding of what it is like to own a Weimaraner but you still need to think about the pros and cons before you decide if it is the right breed for you. You will find a list of pros and cons for the Weimaraner dog breed listed below:

Pros for the Weimaraner Breed

- The Weimaraner is a unique and beautiful breed with a silver-blue coat.
- Weimaraners are generally very healthy and, though they are prone to certain health issues, they have an average lifespan of 11 to 14 years.
- The Weimaraner is a talented and versatile hunting dog – he is skilled with retriever, pointing, and tracking.
- Weimaraners form very close bonds with family and they are extremely loyal.
- The Weimaraner is a fun-loving breed that loves to spend time playing with family – he has a lot of energy.
- Weimaraners become so closely bonded to their owners that they will follow them around the house and can become protective as well, when needed.

Cons for the Weimaraner Breed

- The Weimaraner is a medium-sized breed that can grow up to 90 pounds (41 kg) so they do not do well in apartments and they require outdoor space to run.
- Weimaraners have very thin coats so they do not adapt well to cold environments – they also should not be kept as outdoor dogs.

- The Weimaraner has a strong prey drive and is very likely to chase cats, small dogs, and even small children.
- Weimaraners are intelligent and they need a lot of mental stimulation in addition to physical exercise – they will also require firm, consistent training throughout their lives.
- The Weimaraner is a high-maintenance breed that requires a good deal of daily energy – a short daily walk is not enough for these dogs.
- Weimaraners are very people-oriented and they do not do well when left alone for long periods of time – they are prone to separation anxiety.

Chapter Three: Purchasing Your Weimaraner Dog

If you have officially decided that the Weimaraner is the right breed for you, your next step is to figure out where to get one. In this chapter you will find tips for finding a reputable Weimaraner breeder, as well as thoughts about adopting a rescue dog. You will also find tips for vetting potential breeders, picking out a healthy Weimaraner puppy and puppy-proofing your house. All of these things are part of the process for buying a Weimaraner puppy or adopting an adult dog.

Where Can You Buy Weimaraner Dogs?

Once you have decided that the Weimaraner is definitely the right breed for you, your next task is to find one. Unfortunately, many people think that the best place to find a puppy is at their local pet store. While the puppies at the pet store might look cute and cuddly, there is no way to know whether they are actually healthy or well-bred. Many pet stores get their puppies from puppy mills and they sell the puppies to unsuspecting dog lovers. Puppy mill puppies are often already sick by the time they make it to the pet store, often traveling across state lines to get there.

A puppy mill is a type of breeding facility that focuses on breeding and profit more than the health and wellbeing of the dogs. Puppy mills usually keep their dogs in squalid conditions, forcing them to bear litter after litter of puppies with little to no rest in between. Many of the breeders used in puppy mills are poorly bred themselves or unhealthy to begin with which just ensures that the puppies will have the same problems. The only time you should bring home a puppy from a pet store is if the store has a partnership with a local shelter and that is where they get their dogs.

If the pet store can't tell you which breeder the puppies came from, or if they don't offer you any paperwork or registration for the puppy, it is likely that the puppy came from a puppy mill. Rather than purchasing a Weimaraner puppy from a pet store, your best bet is to find a reputable breeder – preferably and AKC-registered breeder in the United States or a Kennel Club-registered breeder in the U.K. If you visit the website for either of these organizations you can find a list of breeders for all of the club-recognized breeds. You can also check with local, regional, and national breed clubs.

If you don't have your heart set on a Weimaraner puppy, consider adopting a rescue from a local shelter. There are many benefits associated with rescuing an adult dog. For one thing, adoption fees are generally under $200 (£180) which is much more affordable than the $800 to $1,200 (£720 to £1,080) fee to buy a puppy from a breeder. Plus, an adult dog will already be housetrained and may have some obedience training as well. As an added bonus, most shelters spay/neuter their dogs before adopting them out so you won't have to pay for the surgery yourself. Another benefit is that an adult dog has already surpassed the puppy stage so his personality is set – with a puppy you can never quite be sure how your puppy will turn out.

If you are thinking about adopting a Weimaraner, consider one of the breed-specific rescues listed on the following page:

United States Rescues:

Weimaraner Rescue of the South.
<http://www.weimrescue.com/>

Louisville Weimaraner Rescue, Inc.
<http://www.louisvilleweimrescue.com/>

Tri-State Weimaraner Rescue.
<http://tristateweimrescue.com/>

Heartland Weimaraner Rescue.
<http://www.heartlandweimrescue.org/>

Florida Weimaraner Rescue, Inc.
<http://www.flweimrescue.com/>

United Kingdom Rescues:

Independent Weimaraner Rescue & Rehoming Service.
<http://www.weimaraner-rescue.org.uk/>

Weimaraner Club of Great Britain Rescue.
<http://www.weimaranerclubofgreatbritain.org.uk/index.php/rescue/dogs-in-need>

How to Choose a Reputable Weimaraner Breeder

Finding the nearest Weimaraner breeder to your home could be as simple as plugging in some search terms in your Internet browser. You cannot guarantee, however, that the first results will be the best. Take the time to assemble a list of different breeders, drawing on all of your resources such as recommendations from friends or veterinarians, AKC or Kennel Club breeder listings, and Internet search results. Once you have your list of breeders on hand you can go through them one-by-one to narrow down your options. Go through the steps on the following pages to do so:

- Visit the website for each breeder on your list (if they have one) and look for key information about the breeder's history and experience.
    - Check for club registrations and a license, if applicable.
    - If the website doesn't provide any information about the facilities or the breeder you are best just moving on.
- After ruling out some of the breeders, contact the remaining breeders on your list by phone
    - Ask the breeder questions about his experience with breeding dogs in general and about the Weimaraner breed in particular.
    - Ask for information about the breeding stock including registration numbers and health information.
    - Expect a reputable breeder to ask you questions about yourself as well – a responsible breeder wants to make sure that his puppies go to good homes.
- Schedule an appointment to visit the facilities for the remaining breeders on your list after you've weeded a few more of them out.
    - Ask for a tour of the facilities, including the place where the breeding stock is kept as well as the facilities housing the puppies.

- o If things look unorganized or unclean, do not purchase from the breeder.
- o Make sure the breeding stock is in good condition and that the puppies are all healthy-looking and active.
- Narrow down your list to a final few options and then interact with the puppies to make your decision.
  - o Make sure the breeder provides some kind of health guarantee and ask about any vaccinations the puppies may have already received.
- Put down a deposit, if needed, to reserve a puppy if they aren't ready to come home yet.

Tips for Selecting a Healthy Weimaraner Puppy

After you have taken the time to vet several Weimaraner breeders and you have narrowed down your options, you then have to actually go through the process of picking your puppy. It can be tempting to pick the first puppy that comes bounding up to you but you need to be careful about choosing a puppy who is well-bred and in good health. <u>Follow the steps below to pick out your new Weimaraner puppy</u>:

- Ask the breeder to give you a tour of the facilities, especially where the puppies are kept.

- o Make sure the facilities where the puppies are housed is clean and sanitary – if there is evidence of diarrhea, do not purchase one of the puppies because they may already be sick.
- Take a few minutes to observe the litter as a whole, watching how the puppies interact with each other.
  - o The puppies should be active and playful, interacting with each other in a healthy way.
  - o Avoid puppies that appear to be lethargic and those that have difficulty moving – they could be sick.
- Approach the litter and watch how the puppies react to you when you do.
  - o If the puppies appear frightened they may not be properly socialized and you do not want a puppy like that.
  - o The puppies may be somewhat cautious, but they should be curious and interested in you.
- Let the puppies approach you and give them time to sniff and explore you before you interact with them.
  - o Pet the puppies and encourage them to play with a toy, taking the opportunity to observe their personalities.
  - o Single out any of the puppies that you think might be a good fit and spend a little time with them.
- Pick up the puppy and hold him to see how he responds to human contact.

- o The puppy might squirm a little but it shouldn't be frightened of you and it should enjoy being pet.
- Examine the puppy's body for signs of illness and injury
  - o The puppy should have clear, bright eyes with no discharge. The coat should be even and bright white, no patches of hair loss or discoloration.
  - o The ears should be clean and clear with no discharge or inflammation.
  - o The puppy's stomach may be round but it shouldn't be distended or swollen.
  - o The puppy should be able to walk and run normally without any mobility problems.
- Narrow down your options and choose the puppy that you think is the best fit.

Once you've chosen your Weimaraner puppy, ask the breeder about the next steps. Do not take the puppy home if it isn't at least 8 weeks old and unless it has been fully weaned and eating solid food.

Puppy-Proofing Your Home

If you choose to get your Weimaraner puppy from a breeder you may end up picking him out before he is old enough to come home with you. In the meantime, you should plan to prepare your home for your new puppy by puppy-proofing it. Puppy-proofing simply means taking steps to make your home a safe place for your puppy – this may involve putting potentially harmful substances or objects away and installing preventive measures to keep your puppy from getting into things he shouldn't.

On the following page you will find a list of some of the things you should do when you are puppy-proofing your home for your Weimaraner:

- Make sure your trash and recycling containers have a tight-fitting lid or store them in a cabinet - when your puppy grows up he might be big enough to reach into an open trash can.

- Put away all open food containers and keep them out of reach of your puppy – dogs will stop at nothing to get food.

- Store cleaning products and other hazardous chemicals in a locked cabinet or pantry where your puppy can't get them.

- Make sure electrical cords and blind pulls are wrapped up and placed out of your puppy's reach – these things can seem like tantalizing toys to your Weimaraner puppy.

- Pick up any small objects or toys that could be a choking hazard if your puppy chews on them.

- Cover or drain any open bodies of water such as the toilet, and outdoor pond, etc. – even if it doesn't seem like a hazard, it is better to be safe than sorry.

- Store any medications and beauty products in the medicine cabinet out of your puppy's reach.

- Check your home for any plants that might be toxic to dogs and remove them or put them out of reach – you never know when your Weimaraner might get the urge to munch on some leaves.

- Block off fire places, windows, and doors so your puppy can't get into trouble.

- Close off any stairwells and block the entry to rooms where you do not want your puppy to be – this is the best way to keep your puppy out of trouble.

Chapter Four: Caring for Your New Dog

Once you have picked out your Weimaraner puppy and brought him home, you may feel like the hard part is over. The reality is, however, you are just getting started! Becoming a dog owner is a long-term commitment – your Weimaraner will live between 11 and 14 years so you should be prepared to care for him throughout the entire duration of his life. In this chapter you will find tips for setting up your home to your Weimaraner's liking as well as tips for meeting his exercise requirements. Both of these things are essential for keeping your Weimaraner happy.

Habitat and Exercise Requirements for Weimaraner

Even though your Weimaraner puppy may be small at first, he will grow quickly and he could achieve a maximum size of 90 pounds (41 kg). Because Weimaraners can grow fairly large, you should prepare for his adult size from the very beginning. Weimaraners are not recommended for apartment or condo life because they simply need a lot of space. They also need access to the outdoors – preferably a fenced yard – where they can run and play to work off excess energy.

To make sure that your Weimaraner feels at-home, you will need to provide him with certain things. A crate is one of the most important things you will need when you bring your new puppy home. Not only will it be a place for your puppy to sleep, but it will also be a place where you can confine him during the times when you are away from home or when you cannot keep a close eye on him. Crate training is the recommended housetraining method for this breed, so you should get your puppy used to the crate early. Your puppy will also need some other basic things like a water bowl, a food bowl, a collar, a leash, toys, and grooming supplies.

When shopping for food and water bowls, safety and sanitation are the top two considerations. Stainless steel is the best material to go with because it is easy to clean and resistant to bacteria. Ceramic is another good option, though it may be a little heavier. Avoid plastic food and water bowls because they can become scratched and the scratches may harbor bacteria. For your dog's collar and leash, choose one that is appropriate to his size. This may mean that you will purchase several collars and leashes while your puppy is still growing. You might also consider a harness – this will be helpful during leash training because it will improve your control over your puppy and it will distribute pressure across his back instead of putting it all on his throat.

Provide your Weimaraner puppy with an assortment of different toys and let him figure out which ones he likes. Having a variety of toys around the house is very important because you'll need to use them to redirect your puppy's natural chewing behavior as he learns what he is and is not allowed to chew on. As for grooming supplies, you'll need a wire-pin brush for daily brushing. You may also want to purchase some dog nail clippers as well as a dog toothbrush and some dog toothpaste.

In terms of meeting your Weimaraner's needs for exercise, you may need to start out conservatively while your puppy is still young. Adult Weimaraners need a great deal of daily exercise to work off their energy, but vigorous exercise can be dangerous for puppies under 6 months of age. You want to be careful with your Weimaraner puppy's bones and joints while he is still growing in order to protect him from developing musculoskeletal issues later in life. Take your puppy for two or three 15- to 20-minute walks per day until he is six months old, then you can start to make the walks a little longer. Wait until your Weimaraner has reached his maximum size to take him running as a primary form of exercise.

Setting Up Your Puppy's Area

In addition to puppy-proofing your home, before you actually bring your Weimaraner home, you should set up his crate in a particular area of the house that your puppy will be able to call his own. The ideal setup will include your puppy's crate, a comfy dog bed (either in the crate or near it), his food and water bowls, and an assortment of toys. You can arrange all of these items in a small room that is easy to block off or you can use a puppy playpen to give your puppy some free space while still keeping him somewhat confined.

When you bring your Weimaraner puppy home you'll have to work with him a little bit to get him used to the crate. It is very important that you do this because you do not want your puppy to form a negative association with the crate. You want your puppy to learn that the crate is his own special place, a place where he can go to relax and take a nap if he wants to. If you use the crate as punishment, your puppy will not want to use it.

To get your Weimaraner puppy used to the crate, try tossing a few treats into it and let him go fish them out. Feeding your puppy his meals in the crate with the door open will be helpful as well. You can also incorporate the crate into your playtime, tossing toys into the crate or hiding treats under a blanket in the crate. As your puppy gets used to the crate you can start keeping him in it with the door closed for short periods of time, working your way up to longer periods. Just be sure to let your puppy outside before and after you confine him and never force him to stay in the crate for longer than he is physically capable of holding his bowels and his bladder.

Chapter Five: Meeting Your Weimaraner Dog's Nutritional Needs

Choosing a dog food for your Weimaraner may seem as easy as walking into the pet store and grabbing something off the shelf, but it is not. All dog foods are not created equal and the type of food you choose for your dog will have a significant impact on his growth rate as well as his overall health and wellbeing. In this chapter you will learn about your dog's nutritional needs and receive tips for choosing a high-quality dog food. You will also receive general tips for feeding your Weimaraner.

The Nutritional Needs of Dogs

Dogs are widely regarded as carnivorous animals and, while they may not be strict carnivores like cats, their diet should be comprised primarily of protein. Like all living things, however, dogs require a balance of protein, carbohydrate and fat in their diets – this is in addition to essential vitamins and minerals. It is important to understand, however, that your dog's nutritional needs are very different from your own. For dogs, protein is the most important nutritional consideration, followed by fat and then carbohydrates. In order to keep your dog healthy you need to create a diet that provides the optimal levels of these three macronutrients.

The portion of your dog's diet that comes from protein should be made up of animal sources like meat, poultry, and fish as well as meat meals. Protein is made up of amino acids which are the building blocks that make up your Weimaraner's tissues and cells. Protein also provides some energy for your dog. The most highly concentrated type of energy your Weimaraner needs, however, is fat. While fat is something you may have been conditioned to shun, it is a necessary part of your dog's diet.

Though fat is very important for a balanced diet for dogs, you want to make sure that the fat content of your

Weimaraner puppy's diet is not too high. Because fat contains 9 calories per gram (versus 4 calories per gram for protein and carbohydrate), a high fat content correlates to high calorie content. Your Weimaraner puppy needs plenty of protein to fuel his growth and development, but large-breed puppies should be fed a moderate-fat diet to prevent them from growing too quickly. Growing too fast as a puppy can put your adult dog at risk for musculoskeletal problems as an adult or senior dog.

In addition to protein and fat, your Weimaraner also needs carbohydrates to provide dietary fiber and various vitamins and minerals. Dogs do not have a specific need for carbohydrates but they should always come from digestible sources since a dog's digestive tract is not designed to process plant foods as effectively as protein and fat (this is where the carnivore part comes in). Your dog also needs plenty of fresh water on a daily basis as well as key vitamins and minerals. The best way to ensure that your dog's nutritional needs are met is to feed him a diet that is complete and balanced for dogs.

How to Select a High-Quality Dog Food Brand

Shopping for dog food can be overwhelming for new dog owners simply because there are so many different options to choose from. If you walk into your local pet store you will see multiple aisles filled with bags of dog food from different brands and most brands offer a number of different formulas. So how do you choose a healthy dog food for your Weimaraner dog? The best place to start when shopping for dog food is to read the dog food label.

Pet food in the United States is loosely regulated by the American Association of Feed Control Officials (AAFCO) and they evaluate commercial dog food products according to their ability to meet the basic nutritional needs of dogs in various life stages. If the product meets these basic needs, the label will carry some kind of statement from AAFCO like this:

"[Product Name] is formulated to meet the nutritional levels established by the AAFCO Dog Food nutrient profiles for [Life Stage]."

If the dog food product you are looking at contains this statement you can move on to reading the ingredients list. Dog food labels are organized in descending order by volume. This means that the ingredients at the top of the list are used in higher quantities than the ingredients at the end of the list. This being the case, you want to see high-quality sources of animal protein at the beginning of the list. Things like fresh meat, poultry or fish are excellent ingredients but they contain about 80% water. After the product is cooked, the actual volume and protein content of the ingredient will be less. Meat meals (like chicken meal or salmon meal) have already been cooked down so they contain up to 300% more protein by weight than fresh meats.

In addition to high-quality animal proteins, you want to check the ingredients list for digestible carbohydrates and healthy fats. For dogs, digestible carbohydrates include things like brown rice and oatmeal, as long as they have been cooked properly. You can also look for gluten-free and grain-free options like sweet potato and tapioca. It is best to avoid products that are made with corn, wheat, or soy ingredients because they are low in nutritional value and may trigger food allergies in your dog.

In terms of fat, you want to see at least one animal source such as chicken fat or salmon oil. Plant-based fats like flaxseed and canola oil are not necessarily bad, but they are less biologically valuable for your dog. If they are accompanied by an animal source of fat, it is okay. Just make sure that the fats included in the recipe provide a blend of both omega-3 and omega-6 fatty acids. This will help to preserve the quality and condition of your Weimaraner's dog's skin and coat. Just remember to keep the fat content moderate in proportion to the protein content.

In addition to checking the ingredients list for beneficial ingredients you should also know that there are certainly things you do NOT want to see listed. Avoid products made with low-quality fillers like corn gluten meal or rice bran – really any corn, wheat, or soy ingredients should be avoided. You should also avoid artificial colors, flavors, and preservatives. Some commonly used artificial preservatives are BHA and BHT. In most cases the label will tell you if natural preservatives are used.

Tips for Feeding Your Weimaraner

The best way to ensure that your Weimaraner's unique nutritional needs are met is to choose a high-quality dry dog food that is formulated for large-breed puppies. You can feed your puppy this formula as recommended until he reaches about 80% of his projected adult size. Remember, male Weimaraners grow a little larger than females, so you will need to keep this in mind – your vet may be able to give you some idea of your puppy's projected adult size. Once your puppy reaches 80% of his adult size, switch him over to a high-quality dry dog food that is formulated for large-breed adult dogs.

Once you've chosen a healthy diet for your Weimaraner dog you need to know how much and how often to feed him. Because different dog food products have different calorie content you should follow the feeding instructions on the label as a starting point. Most dog food labels provide feeding instructions by weight, so make sure you know how much your puppy weighs. It is also important to remember that these are feeding suggestions – you might have to alter the ration for your dog. If your Weimaraner starts to gain weight, decrease his daily ration a little. If he loses weight, increase it a little bit.

In addition to knowing how much to feed your Weimaraner you also need to think about how often to feed him. Most dog owners recommend feeding your dog twice a day. Puppies need a lot of energy to fuel their growth and development, however, so you may want to divide his daily portion over three small meals. As your Weimaraner puppy is growing you can also go the route of feeding him freely, allowing him to eat as much as he wants. If he starts to grow too quickly, however, you may have to start portioning out his meals. Once he reaches full size, though, you should start rationing his food to make sure he doesn't become overweight.

Dangerous Foods to Avoid

It might be tempting to give in to your dog when he is begging at the table, but certain "people foods" can actually be toxic for your dog. As a general rule, you should never feed your dog anything unless you are 100% sure that it is safe. <u>Below you will find a list of foods that can be toxic to dogs and should therefore be avoided</u>:

- Alcohol
- Apple seeds
- Avocado
- Cherry pits
- Chocolate
- Coffee
- Garlic
- Grapes/raisins
- Hops
- Macadamia nuts
- Mold
- Mushrooms
- Mustard seeds
- Onions/leeks
- Peach pits
- Potato leaves/stems
- Rhubarb leaves
- Tea
- Tomato leaves/stems
- Walnuts
- Xylitol
- Yeast dough

If your Weimaraner eats any of these foods, contact the Pet Poison Control hotline right away at (888) 426 – 4435.

Chapter Six: Training Your Weimaraner

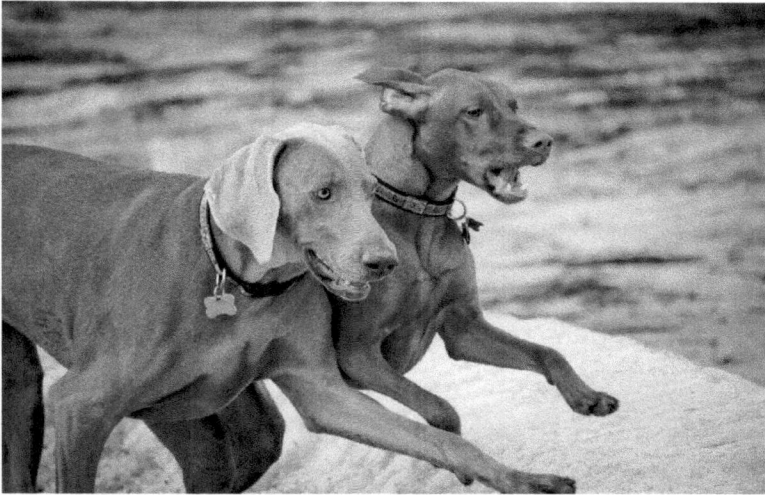

As a dog owner, one of your biggest responsibilities is to train and socialize your Weimaraner. These dogs are notoriously strong-willed at times and they can be a little dog-aggressive – early socialization and training will help to curb these and other behavior problems. There are many different approaches to dog training, but positive reinforcement is generally the most effective for this breed. In this chapter you will receive tips for socializing, training, and housebreaking your Weimaraner puppy.

Socializing Your New Weimaraner Puppy

The Weimaraner was developed as a hunting breed, so these dogs tend to be fairly independent and they can sometimes be strong-willed. For this reason, early socialization is very important. You also want to start socializing your Weimaraner puppy as early as possible because it will increase the likelihood that he will get along with other dogs, household pets, and children. Fortunately, socialization is fairly simple – all you have to do is make sure that he experiences plenty of new people, places, and things during the first few months of his life.

Below you will find a list of things you should expose your Weimaraner puppy to for properly socialization:

- Introduce your puppy to friends in the comfort of your own home.

- Invite friends with dogs or puppies to come meet your puppy (make sure everyone is vaccinated).

- Expose your puppy to people of different sizes, shapes, gender, and skin color.

- Introduce your puppy to children of different ages – just make sure they know how to handle the puppy safely.

- Take your puppy with you in the car when you run errands.

- Walk your puppy in as many places as possible so he is exposed to different surfaces and surroundings.

- Expose your puppy to water from hoses, sprinklers, showers, pools, etc.

- Make sure your puppy experiences loud noises such as fireworks, cars backfiring, loud music, thunder, etc.

- Introduce your puppy to various appliances and tools such as blenders, lawn mowers, vacuums, etc.

- Walk your puppy with different types of harnesses, collars, and leashes.

- Once he is old enough, take your puppy to the dog park to interact with other dogs.

Positive Reinforcement for Obedience Training

The Weimaraner is a very intelligent dog breed that generally responds well to training. Because these dogs have a bit of an independent side, however, training is a lifelong thing – not just something you do with your puppy. Fortunately, training a dog is not as difficult as many people think – it all has to do with the rewards. Think about this – if you want someone do so something for you, you probably offer them something in return. The same concept is true for dog training – if you reward your dog for performing a particular behavior then he will be more likely to repeat it in the future. This is called positive reinforcement training and it is one of the simplest yet most effective training methods you can use as a dog owner.

The key to success with dog training is two-fold. For one thing, you need to make sure that your dog understands what it is you are asking him. If he doesn't know what a command means it doesn't matter how many times you say it, he won't respond correctly. In order to teach your dog what a command means you should give it and then guide him to perform the behavior. Once he does, immediately give him a treat and praise him – the sooner you reward after identifying the desired behavior, the faster your puppy will learn.

The second key to success in dog training is consistency. While your puppy is learning basic obedience commands you need to use the same commands each and every time and you need to be consistent in rewarding him. If you maintain consistency it should only take a few repetitions for your puppy to learn what you expect of him. You can then move on to another command and alternate between them to reinforce your puppy's understanding. Just be sure to keep your training sessions short – about 15 minutes – so your Weimaraner puppy doesn't get bored.

Crate Training - Housebreaking Your Puppy

Although Weimaraners are very smart and trainable, they can also be fairly tricky to housetrain. For the most part, however, it is agreed that crate training is the most effective housetraining method for this breed. The key to house training is to use your puppy's crate appropriately. When you are able to watch your puppy, keep him in the same room with you at all times and take him outdoors once every hour or so to give him a chance to do his business. Always lead him to a particular section of the yard and give him a command like "Go pee" so he learns what is expected of him when you take him to this area.

When you can't watch your puppy and overnight you should confine him to his crate. The crate should be just large enough for your puppy to stand up, sit down, turn around and lie down in. Keeping it this size will ensure that he views the crate as his den and he will be reluctant to soil it. Just make sure that you don't keep your puppy in the crate for longer than he is physically capable of holding his bladder. Always take your puppy out before putting him in the crate and immediately after releasing him.

If you give your puppy ample opportunity to do his business outdoors and you keep him confined to the crate when you can't watch him, housetraining should only take a few weeks. Again, consistency is key here so always reward and praise your puppy for doing his business outside so he learns to do it that way. If your puppy does have an accident, do not punish him because he will not understand – he won't associate the punishment with the crime so he will just learn to fear you instead.

Chapter Seven: Grooming Your Weimaraner

Most Weimaraner owners will agree that the Weimaraner is a high-maintenance breed. You will find that most of your work is concentrated in the areas of training and exercising your dog, however – this breed's short, smooth coat doesn't require a lot of maintenance. In this chapter you will receive some general tips for grooming your Weimaraner's coats as well as recommendations for trimming his nails and brushing his teeth.

Tips for Bathing and Grooming Weimaraner Dogs

Weimaraners have very short coats so you don't need a lot of fancy equipment to keep it in good condition. All you really need to do is bathe your dog when he needs it and brush him a few times a week. To brush your dog's coat, take a wire-pin brush and start at the base of the neck and work your way along the dog's back, down his legs, and under his belly. Always brush in the direction of hair growth and move slowly so you don't hurt your dog if you come across a snag.

If you need to bathe your Weimaraner you will want to brush him first. When you are ready for the bath, fill the bathtub with a few inches of warm (not hot) water and place your dog inside. Use a cup to pour water over your dog's back or use a handheld sprayer to wet down his coat. Once your dog's coat is dampened, apply a small amount of dog-friendly shampoo and work it into a lather. After shampooing, rinse your dog's coat thoroughly to get rid of all the soap and then towel him dry. If it is warm you might be able to let his coat air-dry but if it is cold you should finish it off with a blow dryer on the low heat setting.

Other Grooming Tasks

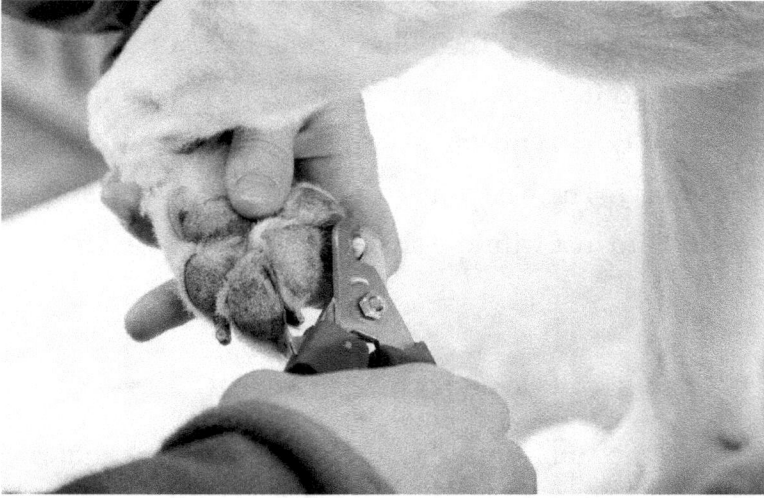

Brushing and bathing your Weimaraner's coat are fairly simple tasks, but there are some other grooming tasks you should stay on top of. For example, you'll need to trim your dog's nails occasionally, clean his ears, and brush his teeth. <u>You will find an overview of each of these dog grooming tasks below</u>:

Trimming Your Weimaraner's Nails

Your dog's nails grow in the same way that your own nails grow so they need to be trimmed occasionally. Most down owners find that trimming their dog's nails once a week or twice a month is sufficient. Before you trim your dog's nails for the first time you should have your veterinarian or a professional groomer show you how to do it. A dog's nail contains a quick – the blood vessel that supplies blood to the nail – and if you cut the nail too short you could sever it. A severed quick will cause your dog pain and it will bleed profusely. The best way to avoid cutting your dog's nails too short is to just trim the sharp tip.

Cleaning Your Weimaraner's Ears

The Weimaraner has drop ears which means that they hang down on either side of the dog's head – they are also fairly large. The large size of the breed's ears and the fact that they hang down reduces airflow to the ear canal and increases the dog's risk for ear infections. If the dog's ears get wet it creates an environment that is beneficial for infection-causing bacteria. Keeping your dog's ears clean and dry is the key to preventing infections – do not get your dog's head wet when you bath him and wash his face carefully with a washcloth if you must wash it. If you have to clean your dog's ears, use a dog ear cleaning solution and squeeze a few drops into the ear canal. Then, massage the base of your dog's ears to distribute the solution then wipe it away using a clean cotton ball.

Brushing Your Weimaraner's Teeth

Many dog owners neglect their dog's dental health which is a serious mistake. Dogs have a high risk for periodontal disease which, if left untreated, can become very severe. You should brush your Weimaraner's teeth with a dog-friendly toothbrush and dog toothpaste at least a few times a week to preserve his dental health. Feeing your dog dental treats and giving him hard rubber toys can also help to maintain his dental health.

Chapter Eight: Breeding Your Weimaraner

You have already learned the importance of responsible breeding for the health of Weimaraner puppies, so it should be clear to you that dog breeding is not a task that should be taken lightly. Not only is it difficult to find breeding stock that are both healthy and disease-free, but you have to care for a pregnant dog as well as her puppies. If you don't plan to breed your Weimaraner, have him or her spayed/neutered before 6 months of age. In addition to preventing unwanted litters, this will help protect your dog against some serious diseases.

Basic Dog Breeding Information

Before you decide whether or not to breed your Weimaraner, you should take the time to learn the basics about dog breeding in general. If you do not want to breed your dog, the ASPCA recommends having him neutered or her spayed before the age of 6 months. For female dogs, six months is around the time the dog experiences her first heat. Heat is just another name for the estrus cycle in dogs and it generally lasts for about 14 to 21 days. The frequency of heat may vary slightly from one dog to another but it generally occurs twice a year. When your female dog goes into heat, this is when she is capable of becoming pregnant.

When a female dog goes into heat there are a few common signs you can look for. The first sign of heat is swelling of the vulva – this may be accompanied by a bloody discharge. Over the course of the heat cycle the discharge lightens in color and becomes more watery. By the 10th day of the cycle the discharge is light pink – this is when she begins to ovulate and it is when she is most fertile. If you plan to breed your Weimaraner, this is when you want to introduce her to the male dog. If the isn't receptive to the male's advances, wait a day or two before trying again.

A dog is technically capable of conceiving at any point during the heat cycle because the male's sperm can survive in her reproductive tract for up to 5 days. If you don't plan to breed your Weimaraner dog you need to keep her locked away while she is in heat. A male dog can smell a female dog in heat from several miles away and an intact male dog will go to great lengths to breed. Never take a female dog in heat to the dog park and be very careful about taking her outside at all. Do not leave her unattended in your backyard because a stray dog could get in and breed with her.

If you want to breed your Weimaraner you will need to keep track of her estrus cycle so you know when to breed her. It generally takes a few years for a dog's cycle to become regular so keep that in mind when you are planning your dog breeding. Keep track of your dog's cycle on a calendar so you know when to breed her. Tracking her cycle and making note of when you introduce her to the male dog will help you predict the due date for the puppies.

Breeding Tips and Raising Puppies

After the male dog fertilizes the egg inside the female dog's body, the female will go through the gestation period during which the puppies start to develop inside her womb. The gestation period for Weimaraner dogs lasts for about 63 days but you won't be able to actually tell that your dog is pregnant until after the third week. By the 25th day of pregnancy it is safe for a vet to perform an ultrasound and by day 28 he should be able to feel the puppies by palpating the female's abdomen. At the six week mark an x-ray can be performed to check the size of the litter.

While the puppies are growing inside your Weimaraner's belly you need to take careful care of her. You don't need to feed your dog any extra until the fourth or fifth week of pregnancy when she really starts to gain weight. Make sure to provide your dog with a healthy diet and keep up with regular vet appointments to make sure the pregnancy is progressing well. Once you reach the fifth week of pregnancy you can increase your dog's daily rations in proportion to her weight gain.

After eight weeks of gestation you should start to get ready for your Weimaraner to give birth – in dogs, this is called whelping. You should provide your dog with a clean, safe, and quiet place to give birth such as a large box in a dimly lit room. Line the box with old towels or newspapers for easy cleanup after the birth and make sure your dog has access to the box at all times. As she nears her due date she will start spending more and more time in the box.

When your Weimaraner is ready to give birth her internal temperature will decrease slightly. If you want to predict when the puppies will be born you can start taking her internal temperature once a day during the last week of gestation. When the dog's body temperature drops from 100°F to 102°F (37.7°C to 38.8°C to about 98°F (36.6°C), labor is likely to begin very soon. At this point your dog will display obvious signs of discomfort such as pacing, panting, or changing positions. Just let her do her own thing but keep an eye on her in case of complications.

During the early stages of labor, your Weimaraner will experience contractions about 10 minutes apart. If she has contractions for more than 2 hours without giving birth, bring her to the vet immediately. Once your dog starts whelping, she will whelp one puppy about every thirty minutes. After every puppy is born, she will clean it with her tongue – this will also help stimulate the puppy to start breathing on its own. After all of the puppies have been born, the mother will expel the afterbirth and the puppies will begin nursing. The litter size for the Weimaraner breed is 6 to 10 with an average of 7 puppies.

It is essential that the puppies start nursing as soon as possible after whelping so that they get the colostrum. The colostrum is the first milk a mother produces and it is loaded with nutrients as well as antibodies that will protect the puppies while their own immune systems continue developing. The puppies will generally start nursing on their own or the mother will encourage them. After the puppies nurse for a little while you should make sure that your mother dog eats something as well.

When they are first born, Weimaraner puppies are very small – they may only weigh between 7 and 10 ounces (200g to 300g). Over the next 7 to 10 days, they will double in size and they will continue growing over the next several months until they zone in on their adult size. When Weimaraner puppies are born they will have some very fine hair but it isn't enough to keep them warm – your mother dog will help with that. The puppies will be born with their eyes and ears closed but they will start to open around the second or third week following birth. Weimaraner puppies are also born with long tails, so you will need to decide whether or not to have them docked.

Your Weimaraner puppies will be heavily dependent on their mother for the first few weeks of life until they start becoming more mobile. Around 5 to 6 weeks of age you should start offering your puppies small amounts of solid food soaked in broth or water to start the weaning process. Over the next few weeks the puppies will start to nurse less and eat more solid food. Around 8 weeks of age they should be completely weaned – this is when they are ready to be separated from their mother.

Chapter Nine: Showing Your Weimaraner

The Weimaraner is a beautiful breed, and certainly one worthy of show. Showing dogs is a major commitment of time and money, however, so you should think carefully before you decide to do it. Before you even decide, you also need to determine whether your Weimaraner is a good specimen for show by comparing him to the breed standard. In this chapter you will find the AKC and Kennel Club standards for the Weimaraner breed as well as some general tips for showing dogs.

Weimaraner Breed Standard

The Weimaraner is a popular breed and one that is recognized by both the AKC in the United States and The Kennel Club in the U.K. The breed standard you need to follow will depend on where you live and in which kind of show you intend to enroll your dog. In the following pages you will find an overview of the Weimaraner breed standard for both the AKC and The Kennel Club.

a.) AKC Weimaraner Standard

General Appearance and Temperament

The Weimaraner is a medium-sized gray dog, presenting a good example of speed, stamina, balance, and alertness. His conformation should, above all else, indicate a strong working ability and great field endurance.

Head and Neck

The head is moderately long with a moderate stop and a slight median line extending backward over the forehead. The neck is moderately long and clean-cut, the expression kind and intelligent. The ears are long, set high, and slightly folded. The eyes are light amber, blue-gray, or gray and set well apart. The nose is gray, the lips pinkish. A pink nose is considered a minor fault.

Body and Tail

The back is moderate in length and set in a straight line, sloping slightly at the withers. The chest is deep with well sprung ribs and a firmly held abdomen. The tail is docked to approximately 6 inches in length and carried in a confident manner. Non-docked tails will be penalized.

Legs and Feet

The forelegs are straight and strong, the hindquarters well-angulated with straight hocks. The muscles are well developed, the feet firm and compact. The toes are well arched and webbed, the nails short and gray.

Coat and Color

The coat is short, smooth and sleek with solid color in shades of mouse-gray to silver-gray, blending with lighter shades on the head and ears. Small white markings on the chest are allowed but will be penalized on any other part of the body. A long coat is a disqualification as is a distinctly blue or black coat.

Size

Dogs should be 25 to 27 inches at the withers and bitches 23 to 25 inches. Dogs measuring less than 24 inches or more than 28 inches and bitches under 22 inches or over 26 inches will be disqualified.

Gait

The gait is smooth and effortless. When viewed from the rear, the hind feet are parallel to the front and, when viewed from the side, the topline remains strong and level.

b.) The Kennel Club Weimaraner Standard

General Appearance and Temperament

The Weimaraner is a medium-sized gray dog with light-colored eyes. The dog presents a picture of stamina, power, and balance.

Head and Neck

The head is moderately long and aristocratic with a moderate stop and a slight median line extending backward over the forehead. The neck is moderately long and clean-cut. The foreface is straight and delicate at the nostrils, the skin tightly drawn. The eyes are medium-sized in shades of amber or blue-grey and set widely apart. The ears are long and lobular, set high and slightly folded.

Body and Tail

The body is greater in length from point of shoulder to point of buttock than the height at the withers, approximately in 12:10 proportion. The chest is deep and well developed, the topline level, and the ribs well sprung. The tail is previously customarily docked so that the remaining tail is long enough to cover the scrotum in dogs and the vulva in bitches. For undocked tails, the thickness should be in proportion to the body, reaching down to the hocks and tapering at the tip. The tail should be carried below the level of the back when relaxed and raised when animated, not curled over the back.

Legs and Feet

The forelegs are strong and straight, equal in measurement from the elbow to the ground and the elbow to the top of the withers. The hindquarters are moderately angulated and well-muscled. The feet are firm and compact, the toes well arched with close, thick pads.

Coat and Color

The coat is short, smooth and sleek except in the longhaired variety which is 2.5-5 cm long on the body and somewhat longer on the neck, belly and chest. The only correct color is grey, with silver-grey being preferable. Shades of mouse gray are acceptable and the color may blend into lighter shades on the head and ears.

Size

Dogs shall be 61 to 29 cm at the withers and bitches 56 to 65 cm at the withers.

Gait

The gait is effortless and smooth. When viewed from the rear, the hind feet are parallel to the front and, when viewed from the side, the topline remains strong and level.

Preparing Your Weimaraner for Show

After you've reviewed the Weimaraner breed standard and have determined that your dog is a good specimen, you can start thinking about actually entering him into an AKC or Kennel Club show. Dog shows happen all year round and each show is unique, so check your local listings to find one in your area. The rules for each show are different, but there are some general rules you should be prepared to follow.

In the following pages you will find a list of some general and specific recommendations to follow during show prep:

- Make sure that your Weimaraner is properly socialized to be in an environment with many other dogs and people.

- Ensure that your Weimaraner is completely housetrained and able to hold his bladder for at least several hours.

- Solidify your dog's grasp of basic obedience – he should listen and follow basic commands.

- Do some research to learn the requirements for specific shows before you choose one – make sure your dog meets all the requirements for registration.

- Make sure that your Weimaraner is caught up on his vaccinations (especially Bordetella since he will be around other dogs) and have your vet clear his overall health for show.

- Have your dog groomed about a week before the show and then take the necessary steps to keep his coat clean and in good condition.

In addition to making sure that your Weimaraner meets the requirements for the show and is a good representation of the breed standard, you should also pack a bag of supplies that you will need on the day of show. <u>Below you will find a list of helpful things to include in your dog show supply pack</u>:

- Registration information
- Dog crate or exercise pen
- Grooming table and grooming supplies
- Food and treats
- Food and water bowls
- Trash bags
- Medication (if needed)
- Change of clothes
- Food/water for self
- Paper towels or rags
- Toys for the dog

If you want to show your Weimaraner but you don't want to jump immediately into an AKC or Kennel Club show, you may be able to find some local dog shows in your area. Local shows may be put on by a branch of a national Weimaraner breed club and they can be a great place to learn and to connect with other Weimaraner owners.

Chapter Ten: Keeping Your Weimaraner Dog Healthy

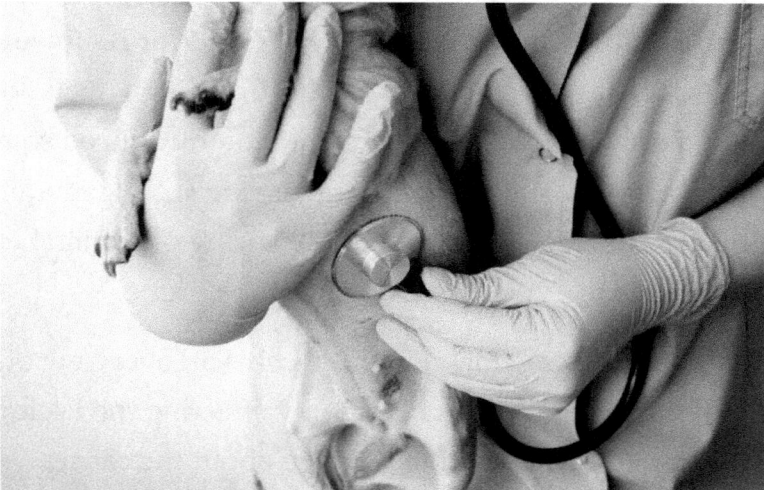

It won't take long for your Weimaraner to become a member of the family and, as such, you will want to take the best care of him you possibly can. Not only does this mean meeting his needs for exercise and healthy food, but you will also have to do certain things to keep him in good health. You should take your Weimaraner to the vet at least once a year and keep him up to date on vaccinations. In this chapter you will learn about health issues common to the breed and about the vaccines your dog might need.

Common Health Problems Affecting Weimaraner Dogs

The Weimaraner dog breed was developed during the early 19th century from a large pool of various hunting and pointing breeds. Following World War II, however, there was a surge of irresponsible breeding which not only tainted the breed's temperament, but introduced some health issues as well. Weimaraners are still a generally healthy breed, but you should be aware of certain health problems to which these dogs may be prone.

In this section you will receive an overview of some of the conditions most commonly affecting the Weimaraner dog breed. By educating yourself about the cause, presentation, and treatment for these common conditions you can help to keep your dog in good health for as long as possible. Some of the common conditions affecting Weimaraner dogs include:

- Distichiasis
- Entropion
- Gastric Dilation Volvulus
- Hip Dysplasia
- Hypertrophic Osteodystrophy
- Hypothyroidism
- Progressive Retinal Atrophy
- Skin Allergies

- Von Willebrand's Disease

In the following pages you will receive an overview of each of these conditions including the symptoms to look for, the causes, and the most common treatment options for the various conditions listed.

Distichiasis

Distichiasis is an eye problem that specifically affects the dog's eyelashes. This condition occurs when small eyelashes grow from the inner surface or the edge of the eyelids – places where they normally do not grow. This condition can affect both the upper and lower lid and it causes severe irritation of the cornea as the hairs rub against it. The affected eye generally becomes red and inflamed – it may also develop a discharge. Dogs with distichiasis may be seen to squint, blink frequently, or run their eye.

In the early stages, distichiasis causes minor irritation but, if left untreated, it can lead to severe corneal ulceration and even infection of the eye. If the itching becomes extreme, the dog may actually injure himself trying to rub or scratch his eye against objects. In the case of severe infections, the dog could also go blind. Treatment generally involves removal of the eyelashes via surgery or electroepilation. Electroepilation involves inserting a tiny needle into the hair follicle and discharging and electric current to kill the hair at the root. The dog may also require antibiotic eye drops following treatment to eliminate post-surgical infection.

Entropion

This is a genetic condition in dogs which affects a portion of the eyelid to become inverted or to fold inward. As the eyelid rolls inward, the eyelashes may rub against the surface of the eye causing minor irritation at first but eventually leading to corneal ulceration or perforation if left untreated. Over time, the irritation may also lead to the development of scar tissue over the wound which could have an effect on the dog's vision. This condition can affect any breed, but it is most commonly seen in large and sporting breeds like the Weimaraner.

Entropion is often caused by abnormal facial anatomy such as a shortened facial structure in brachycephalic breeds. In large-breed dogs, however, you have the opposite problem – excess slack in the ligaments near the outer corer of the eyes which allows the outer edges of the lid to roll inward. Symptoms of entropion include excessive tearing, inflammation of the inner eye, and mucus or discharge from the eye. Treatment typically involves lubricating eye drops and/or surgery to correct the eyelid's position. After treatment the dog may also need antibiotic eye drops.

Gastric Dilation Volvulus

Also known as bloat or gastric torsion, gastric dilation volvulus is a condition that most commonly affects large and deep-chested breeds. This condition occurs when the animal's stomach fills with air and it twists on its axis, cutting off blood flow to and from the stomach. As the condition progresses, the abdomen fills with air and the organs and systems in the dog's body begin to break down from lack of oxygen and blood flow.

Some of the most common symptoms of gastric torsion in dogs include anxiety, depression, and abdominal pain or distended abdomen. Your dog may also start to drool excessively or vomit repeatedly. If the condition isn't corrected, his heart beat will become rapid and he will have trouble breathing. His pulse will weaken and he may fall into a coma or die suddenly.

The exact cause for this condition is unknown but certain things may increase the risk such as consuming large amounts of food or water in a short period of time. Strenuous exercise following a meal or swallowing too much air while eating can lead to gastric torsion as well. Immediate treatment is required to prevent death and surgical options are the most effective. Once treated, most dogs recover within a few weeks.

Hip Dysplasia

Hip dysplasia is a very common musculoskeletal problem among dogs. In a normal hip, the head of the femur (thigh bone) sits snugly within the groove of the hip joint and it rotates freely within the grove as the dog moves. Hip dysplasia occurs when the femoral head becomes separated from the hip joint – this is called subluxation. This could occur as a result of abnormal joint structure or laxity in the muscles and ligaments supporting the joint.

This condition can present in puppies as young as 5 months of age or in older dogs. The most common symptoms of hip dysplasia include pain or discomfort, limping, hopping, or unwillingness to move. As the condition progresses, the dog's pain will increase and he may develop osteoarthritis. The dog may begin to lose muscle tone and might even become completely lame in the affected joint.

Genetics are the largest risk factor for hip dysplasia, though nutrition and exercise are factors as well. Diagnosis for hip dysplasia is made through a combination of clinical signs, physical exam, and x-rays. Surgical treatments for hip dysplasia are very common and generally highly effective. Medical treatments may also be helpful to reduce osteoarthritis and to manage pain.

Hypertrophic Osteodystrophy

Also known as HOD, hypertrophic osteodystrophy is a type of bone disease that most commonly affects large, fast-growing dog breeds like the Weimaraner. The cause of this disease is not known but there are several theories. One theory suggests that the disease is caused by a bacterial infection that leads to high fever and changes in the bone. It may also be that vitamin C deficiency increases the risk for this disease. In any case, it most commonly strikes between 3 and 6 months of age and it is more commonly seen in male puppies than in female puppies.

Dogs that develop HOD typically exhibit signs of mild to moderate pain and swelling in the growth plates in their legs. The bones most commonly affected include the ulna, radius, and tibia. As the condition develops, your dog may show signs of lameness or a general reluctance to move – he may also become lethargic and uninterested in food. Fevers often occur with this disease and the symptoms may wax and wane. Some dogs with HOD suffer permanent bone damage or even die. Because the cause is unknown, there is no cure – treatments are generally supportive in nature, such as anti-inflammatories and pain-killers.

Hypothyroidism

This condition is very common in dogs and it can produce a wide variety of symptoms. Hypothyroidism occurs when the thyroid gland fails to produce enough thyroid hormone – this often leads to weigh loss as well as hair and skin problems. Fortunately, this condition is easy to diagnose with a blood test that checks the dog's levels of certain thyroid hormones like T4.

The thyroid is a gland located in your dog's neck close to the voice box, or larynx. The activity of the thyroid is regulated by the pituitary gland in the brain which produces thyroid stimulating hormone (TSH). Hypothyroidism occurs when the thyroid produces insufficient thyroid hormone – this is most often caused by a destruction of the thyroid gland. This is often associated with other diseases like cancer or atrophy of the thyroid tissue. The use of certain medications can affect the thyroid gland as well.

Hypothyroidism is most commonly diagnosed in dogs between 4 and 10 years of age. The main symptoms of this disease include lethargy, hair loss, weight gain, excessive shedding, hyperpigmentation of skin, slow heartrate, high blood cholesterol and anemia. Treatment usually involves daily treatment with synthetic thyroid hormone.

Progressive Retinal Atrophy

The Weimaraner breed is prone to several different eye problems including progressive retinal atrophy, also known as PRA. This is a degenerative disease that affects the retina of the eye – the part of the eye that is sensitive to light. PRA generally occurs in both eyes at the same time and it may lead to total blindness, though it is not painful for the dog. In fact, many dogs adapt well to a loss of vision as long as furniture and objects are kept in the same location around the home.

There are several forms of PRA characterized by the age of onset and the rate of progression. In most dogs, the photoreceptors in the retina of the eye develop around 8 weeks of age. If the dog has PRA, the retinas might not develop as well or they could begin degenerating at this point. Dogs with PRA generally experience degeneration within two months of birth and most of them go completely blind within a year.

Though PRA is not painful for your dog, it does affect his ability to see. The outward appearance of the eye is generally normal (no tearing or inflammation) but you might notice signs of changing vision. For example, the dog might have trouble seeing at night or it might be reluctant to go down stairs. Eventually the pupil will become dilated and, in some cases, the lens becomes cloudy or opaque.

Skin Allergies

Just like humans, dogs can develop allergic reactions to a number of different things including medications, certain foods, dust, and other environmental pollutants. An allergy develops when the dog's immune system identifies a substance as pathogenic, or dangerous, and it launches an attack. Allergens can be inhaled, ingested, or taken into the body through skin contact. Dogs can develop allergies at any time and some breeds are more prone to allergies than others. The best treatment for allergies is avoiding contact with the allergen. For some environmental allergens, your vet might prescribe antihistamines or your vet might give your dog an injection to protect him.

Common symptoms of allergies in dogs including red or itchy skin, runny eyes, increased scratching, ear infections, sneezing, vomiting, diarrhea, and swollen paws. Some common allergens for dogs include smoke, pollen, mold, dust, dander, feathers, fleas, medications, cleaning products, certain fabrics, and certain foods. Surprisingly, food allergies tend to produce skin-related symptoms like itching and scratching rather than digestive symptoms. Chronic ear infections are also a common sign of food allergies in dogs.

Von Willebrand's Disease

Von Willebrand's disease (or vWD) is a disease of the blood that affects certain dog breeds more than others. This disease is caused a deficiency of von Willebrand Factor (vWF) in the dog's blood. Von Willebrand Factor is a type of adhesive glycoprotein found in the blood which is required for normal platelet binding, or clotting. Lack of vWF can lead to excessive bleeding following even a minor injury. It may also cause nosebleeds, bloody urine, bloody stool, bleeding gums, and vaginal bleeding (in females). It can also cause bruising and anemia.

This disease is an inherited condition caused by genetic mutations that affect the synthesis, release and stability of vWF. In order to diagnose vWD, your veterinarian will perform a physical exam as well as a medical history. Blood count and blood chemical profiles will also be obtained along with a urinalysis and electrolyte panel. The best treatment for von Willebrand's Disease is transfusion with fresh plasma and fresh blood to increase the supply of vWF in the blood. Fortunately, this condition can be managed in mild to moderate cases. Dogs with more severe vWD may require additional transfusions for surgery and supportive care may be required following spontaneous bleeding episodes.

Error! Bookmark not defined.

Preventing Illness with Vaccinations

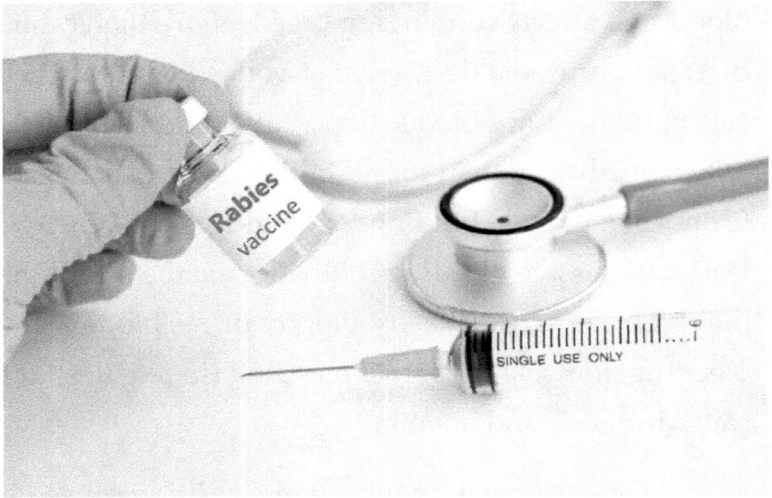

The two most important things you can to do keep your Weimaraner healthy are to give him a healthy diet and keep up with his routine vet visits. You also shouldn't overlook the importance of annual vaccinations. Having your dog vaccinated will help to protect him from deadly diseases like rabies, distemper, and parvovirus. The vaccines your Weimaraner needs may vary depending where you live since certain regions have a higher risk for certain diseases. Your vet will know which vaccinations your dog needs and when he needs them and the vaccination schedule below will give you an idea what you should expect.

To give you an idea what kind of vaccinations your puppy will need, consult the vaccination schedule below:

Vaccination Schedule for Dogs**			
Vaccine	**Doses**	**Age**	**Booster**
Rabies	1	12 weeks	annual
Distemper	3	6-16 weeks	3 years
Parvovirus	3	6-16 weeks	3 years
Adenovirus	3	6-16 weeks	3 years
Parainfluenza	3	6 weeks, 12-14 weeks	3 years
Bordetella	1	6 weeks	annual
Lyme Disease	2	9, 13-14 weeks	annual
Leptospirosis	2	12 and 16 weeks	annual
Canine Influenza	2	6-8, 8-12 weeks	annual

** Keep in mind that vaccine requirements may vary from one region to another. Only your vet will be able to tell you which vaccines are most important for the region where you live.

Weimaraner Care Sheet

After finishing this book you should have a thorough understanding of the Weimaraner breed as well as a good idea whether or not it is the right breed for you. As you enter the world of dog ownership, you may find that you still have questions or that you need to reference key facts and pieces of information about the breed. Rather than flipping through the whole book to find the answers, in this chapter you will find a compilation of the most important information about the Weimaraner organized in a handy care sheet.

1.) Basic Weimaraner Information

Pedigree: developed during the 19th century from various breeds including the Bloodhound, English Pointer, German Shorthaired Pointer and the blue Great Dane

AKC Group: Sporting Group

Breed Size: Medium

Height: 23 to 27 inches (58.5 to 68.5 cm)

Weight: 55 to 90 pounds (25 to 41 kg)

Coat Length: short

Coat Texture: coarse, hard and smooth

Color: silver-grey is most common but may range from charcoal-blue to blue-grey or even mouse-grey

Eyes and Nose: grey, blue-grey, or amber

Ears: drop ears; large, very thin

Tail: traditionally docked to maximum of 6 inches (15.2 cm); may be left natural; long and whip-like

Temperament: high-energy, intelligent, independent, high-strung, people-oriented

Strangers: often suspicious of strangers and may act aggressively unless they are trained and socialized from an early age

Children: may not be a good choice for young children; can get along with other children who are accustomed to dogs

Other Dogs: depends on the dog; some have a low tolerance for other dogs (especially small dogs) but this problem can often be remedied with training and socialization if started at an early age

Training: intelligent and very trainable; they can learn quickly but need constant stimulation to avoid boredom; prone to separation anxiety

Exercise Needs: bred for excellent stamina and endurance so they have high exercise needs; brisk daily jog is recommended along with time to run in a fenced yard

Health Conditions: hip dysplasia, gastric dilation volvulus, von Willebrand's Disease, distichiasis, entropion, hypothyroidism, progressive retinal atrophy, skin allergies

Lifespan: average 11 to 14 years

2.) Weimaraner Habitat Requirements

Recommended Accessories: crate, dog bed, food/water dishes, toys, collar, leash, harness, grooming supplies

Collar and Harness: sized by weight

Grooming Supplies: wire pin brush, dog nail clippers, dog toothbrush and toothpaste

Grooming Frequency: brush daily; professional grooming once or twice a year

Energy Level: very high

Exercise Requirements: two to three 15- to 20-minut walks daily for puppies up to 6 months; increase length of walks up to one year; consider running with dog after 1 year

Crate: highly recommended

Crate Size: just large enough for puppy to lie down and turn around comfortably

Crate Extras: lined with blanket or plush pet bed

Food/Water: stainless steel or ceramic bowls, clean daily

Toys: start with an assortment, see what the dog likes; include some mentally stimulating toys

Exercise Ideas: play games to give your dog extra exercise during the day; train your dog for various dog sports

3.) Basic Dog Nutritional Needs

Nutritional Needs: water, protein, carbohydrate, fats, vitamins, minerals

Calorie Needs: varies by age, weight, and activity level

Amount to Feed (puppy): feed freely but consult recommendations on the package

Amount to Feed (adult): consult recommendations on the package; calculated by weight

Feeding Frequency: two to three meals daily

Important Ingredients: fresh animal protein (chicken, beef, lamb, turkey, eggs), digestible carbohydrates (rice, oats, barley), animal fats

Important Minerals: calcium, phosphorus, potassium, magnesium, iron, copper and manganese

Important Vitamins: Vitamin A, Vitamin A, Vitamin B-12, Vitamin D, Vitamin C

Look For: AAFCO statement of nutritional adequacy; protein at top of ingredients list; avoid corn, wheat and soy ingredients; no artificial flavors, dyes, preservatives

4.) Breeding Information

Age of First Heat: around 6 months (or earlier)

Heat (Estrus) Cycle: 14 to 21 days

Frequency: twice a year, every 6 to 7 months

Greatest Fertility: 11 to 15 days into the cycle

Gestation Period: average 63 days

Pregnancy Detection: possible after 21 days, best to wait 28 days before exam

Feeding Pregnant Dogs: maintain normal diet until week 5 or 6 then slightly increase rations

Signs of Labor: body temperature drops below normal 100° to 102°F (37.7° to 38.8°C), may be as low as 98°F (36.6°C); dog begins nesting in a dark, quiet place

Contractions: period of 10 minutes in waves of 3 to 5 followed by a period of rest

Whelping: puppies are born in 1/2 hour increments following 10 to 30 minutes of forceful straining

Puppies: born with eyes and ears closed; eyes open at 3 weeks, teeth develop at 10 weeks

Litter Size: between 6 and 10 puppies, average 7

Size at Birth: between 7 and 10 ounces (200g to 300g)

Weaning: start offering puppy food soaked in water at 5 to 6 weeks; fully weaned by 8 weeks

Socialization: start as early as possible to prevent puppies from being nervous as an adult

Index

C

F

G

H

I

protein	55, 56, 58, 110
puppies	5, 7, 36, 40, 41, 42, 43, 65, 78, 79, 80, 81, 82, 111, 112
puppy	31, 110, 112, 122, 123, 124
puppy mill	36
puppy playpen	52
puppy-proofing	35, 45, 52, 124
purebred	3, 10, 25

R

rabies	19, 104
record	6
registry	3
retrieving	3, 1, 126
reward	67, 68, 70

S

safety	49
scenting	15
separation anxiety	2, 11, 13, 22, 34, 108
sex	28
shampoo	72
shedding	10, 30, 100
shelter	27, 36, 37
show	3, 10, 16, 74, 83, 84, 89, 90, 91, 99
sire	4, 6
size	23, 26, 49, 50, 51, 60, 61, 69, 74, 79, 81
skin	4, 6, 10, 12, 14, 27, 30, 59, 65, 87, 100, 102, 108
skull	3
social	21
socialization	3, 2, 11, 13, 21, 23, 64, 65, 108
spay	5, 25, 28
stamina	3, 1, 10, 14, 15, 84, 86, 108
standard	91

W

References

"AAFCO Dog Food Nutrient Profiles." DogFoodAdvisor. <http://www.dogfoodadvisor.com/frequently-asked-questions/aafco-nutrient-profiles/>

"Abnormal Eyelid in Dogs." PetMD. <http://www.petmd.com/dog/conditions/eyes/c_multi_entropion?page=2>

"Annual Dog Care Costs." PetFinder. <https://www.petfinder.com/pet-adoption/dog-adoption/annual-dog-care-costs/>

"Are We Breeding Too Many Weimaraners?" Friends for Pets Foundation. <http://www.friendsforpets.org/breeding.php>

"Breed Standard." The Kennel Club. <http://www.thekennelclub.org.uk/services/public/breed/standard.aspx?id=2058>

"Canine Dental Disease." Banfield Pet Hospital. <http://www.banfield.com/pet-health-resources/preventive-care/dental/canine-dental-disease>

"Choosing a Healthy Puppy." WebMD. <http://pets.webmd.com/dogs/guide/choosing-healthy-puppy>

"Distichiasis: Eyelashes Irritating the Eye in Dogs."
PetEducation.com. <http://www.peteducation.com/
article.cfm?c=2+2092&aid=420>

"Feeding the Weimaraner." Wyheestar Weimaraners.
<https://owyheestarweimaranersnews.com/2013/02/22/feed
ing-the-weimar/>

"How to Find a Responsible Breeder." HumaneSociety.org.
<http://www.humanesociety.org/issues/puppy_mills/tips/f
inding_responsible_dog_breeder.html?referrer=https://ww
w.google.com/>

"Hypertrophic Osteodystrophy: A Bone Disease in Growing
Dogs." PetEducation.com. <http://www.peteducation.com/
article.cfm?c=2+2084&aid=446>

"Most Popular Dog Breeds in America." AKC.org.
<http://www.akc.org/news/the-most-popular-dog-breeds-
in-america/>

"My Bowl: What Goes into a Balanced Diet for Your Dog?"
PetMD. <http://www.petmd.com/dog/slideshows/
nutrition-center/my-bowl-what-goes-into-a-balanced-diet-
for-your-dog>

"Nutrients Your Dog Needs." ASPCA.org.
<https://www.aspca.org/pet-care/dog-care/nutrients-your-
dog-needs>

"Nutrition: General Feeding Guidelines for Dogs." VCA
Animal Hospitals. <http://www.vcahospitals.com/

main/pet-health-information/article/animal-health/nutrition-general-feeding-guidelines-for-dogs/6491>

"Official Standard of the Weimaraner." AKC.org. <http://images.akc.org/pdf/breeds/standards/Weimaraner.pdf?_ga=1.55955115.1868964922.1472221340>

"Pet Care Costs." ASPCA.org. <https://www.aspca.org/adopt/pet-care-costs>

"Puppy Proofing Your Home." Hill's Pet. <http://www.hillspet.com/dog-care/puppy-proofing-your-home.html>

"Puppy Proofing Your Home." PetEducation.com. <http://www.peteducation.com/article.cfm?c=2+2106&aid=3283>

"The Weimaraner." The American Kennel Club. <http://www.akc.org/dog-breeds/weimaraner/>

Vitamins and Minerals Your Dog Needs." Kim Boatman. The Dog Daily. <http://www.thedogdaily.com/dish/diet/dogs_vitamins/index.html#.VHOtMPnF_IA>

"Weimaraner." Dog Breed Information Center. <http://www.dogbreedinfo.com/weimaraner.htm>

"Weimaraner." Dogtime.com. <http://dogtime.com/dog-breeds/weimaraner#/slide/1>

"Weimaraner." PetMD. <http://www.petmd.com/dog/breeds/c_dg_weimaraner>

"Weimaraner." VetStreet.com. <http://www.vetstreet.com/dogs/weimaraner#personality>

"Weimaraner Health Problems." Barrett Weimaraners. <http://www.barrettweimaraners.com/weimaraner-health-problems/>

"What is Normal for A Newborn Puppy?" Veterinary Expert. <http://www.theveterinaryexpert.com/general-interest/newborn-puppy/>

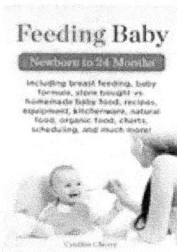

Feeding Baby
Cynthia Cherry
978-1941070000

Axolotl
Lolly Brown
978-0989658430

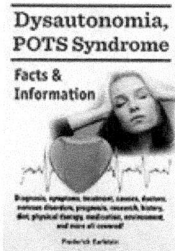

Dysautonomia, POTS
Syndrome
Frederick Earlstein
978-0989658485

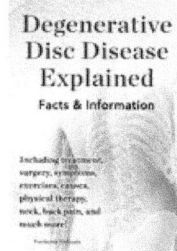

Degenerative Disc
Disease Explained
Frederick Earlstein
978-0989658485

Sinusitis, Hay Fever,
Allergic Rhinitis Explained
Frederick Earlstein
978-1941070024

Wicca
Riley Star
978-1941070130

Zombie Apocalypse
Rex Cutty
978-1941070154

Capybara
Lolly Brown
978-1941070062

Eels As Pets
Lolly Brown
978-1941070167

Scabies and Lice Explained
Frederick Earlstein
978-1941070017

Saltwater Fish As Pets
Lolly Brown
978-0989658461

Torticollis Explained
Frederick Earlstein
978-1941070055

Kennel Cough
Lolly Brown
978-0989658409

Physiotherapist, Physical
Therapist
Christopher Wright
978-0989658492

Rats, Mice, and Dormice
As Pets
Lolly Brown
978-1941070079

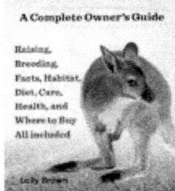

Wallaby and Wallaroo Care
Lolly Brown
978-1941070031

Bodybuilding Supplements Explained
Jon Shelton
978-1941070239

Demonology
Riley Star
978-19401070314

Pigeon Racing
Lolly Brown
978-1941070307

Dwarf Hamster
Lolly Brown
978-1941070390

Cryptozoology
Rex Cutty
978-1941070406

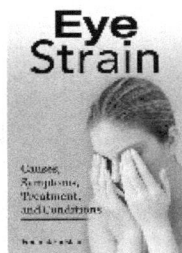

Eye Strain
Frederick Earlstein
978-1941070369

Inez The Miniature Elephant
Asher Ray
978-1941070353

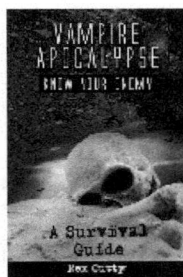

Vampire Apocalypse
Rex Cutty
978-1941070321

www.ingramcontent.com/pod-product-compliance
Lightning Source LLC
LaVergne TN
LVHW051643080426
835511LV00016B/2455